101 Ar
L

© 2018 101 Amazing Things

All rights reserved. No part of this publication may be reproduced, distributed, or transmitted in any form or by any means, including photocopying, recording, or other electronic or mechanical methods, without the prior written permission of the publisher, except in the case of brief quotations embodied in critical reviews and certain other noncommercial uses permitted by copyright law.

Introduction

So you're going to Spain, huh? You are very lucky indeed! You are sure in for a treat because Spain is, without a doubt, one of the most special travel destinations on the face of the planet. It offers something for every visitor, so whether you are into exploring incredible Spanish wines, topping up your tan on one of the many stunning beaches, or discovering the ancient Moorish palaces of Andalucía, Spain has something for every kind of traveller.

This guide will take you on a journey from the major cities like Madrid, Barcelona, Seville, Granada, and Valencia as well some of the less visited places such as Bilbao, Cadiz, Cordoba, Malaga, the Basque Country, and even some of the Spanish islands like Lanzarote and Formentera.

In this guide, we'll be giving you the low down on:
- the very best things to shove in your pie hole, whether you want to have a decadent experience at the world's oldest restaurant in Madrid, or you fancy having a pint at a traditional cider house in the Basque Country

- incredible festivals, from electronic festivals in the middle of a desert, through to street parties at which you throw tomatoes at strangers
- the coolest historical and cultural sights that you simply cannot afford to miss like the sumptuous Alhambra in Granada, and Seville Cathedral, the largest Gothic cathedral in the whole world
- the most incredible outdoor adventures, whether you want to have a snorkelling adventure in the waters of a remote island, or you fancy testing out your skills on the ski slopes just outside of Madrid
- where to shop for authentic souvenirs so that you can remember your trip to Spain forever
- the places where you can party like a local and make new friends
- and tonnes more coolness besides!

Let's not waste any more time – here are the 101 most amazing, spectacular, and coolest things not to miss in Spain!

1. Immerse Yourself in Art at the Museo Del Prado

To say that there is a vibrant arts culture in Madrid is an understatement. This city is a major player on the global stage when it comes to the arts, and the most acclaimed gallery in the city is Museo del Prado. The collection of European art here is simply one of the finest in Europe with over 7600 paintings, 4800 prints, 8000 drawings, and 1000 sculptures. Works from the likes of Goya, Valezquez, and Rembrandt, amongst many others are in the permanent collection. An absolute must for art lovers.
(Paseo del Prado, Madrid; www.museodelprado.es/en)

2. Visit One of the World's Largest Churches, Seville Cathedral

It's a well known fact that Europe is the place to visit if you want to see grand church architecture, but there are churches and then there are churches. Seville Cathedral just so happens to be one of the most special feats of religious architecture we have ever seen up close. Completed in the early 16th century, it is the third largest church and the largest Gothic cathedral anywhere in the world. You can spend multiple days exploring all of the design details and intricacies. Christopher Columbus also happens to be buried there.

(Av. de la Constitución, s/n, 41004 Sevilla; www.catedraldesevilla.es)

3. Jump the Bonfires of Arizkun Carnival

Spain is most certainly a country where the people love to celebrate and occasionally throw a party in the street, but truthfully, we have never seen festivities quite like the Arizkun Carnival. This is a festival that only takes place up in the Basque country in the town of Arizkun, and the basic idea is that on Midsummer night many bonfires are lit, and you have to jump over the bonfires. This apparently dates back to Pagan times when this ritual was enacted to ward off evil spirits and encourage fertility.

4. Take in the Views From a 9th Century Castle in Alicante

Alicante is a charming place on the Iberian coast where many Europeans and local holidaymakers alike choose to spend their free time relaxing on the beach and enjoying quiet coastal life. But there's also some history and culture to be found at Alicante, and the Santa Barbara Castle is a very unique sight indeed because it has been built on the edge of a huge cliff. Fortunately, there is a lift through the mountain to take you to the top, where you'll have an incredible panorama.

(www.castillodesantabarbara.com)

5. Hit the Ski Slopes at Valdesqui

When you think of Madrid, you probably don't think of it as a ski destination. Sure, it's not the Swiss Alps, but if you've ever visited the Spanish capital in the winter months, you'll know how chilly it can get, and there are mountain ranges just outside of the city. In fact, Valdesqui, a ski range in the Guadarrama mountain range is just about an hour's drive from Madrid. There are 29 pistes of varying difficulties so that complete beginners to advanced skiers can enjoy the slopes.

(Puerto de Cotos Carretera s/n, 28740 Rascafría; www.valdesqui.es)

6. Party Hard in the Spanish Desert

If you are the kind of person who loves to party hard, there's no doubt that you will have an awesome time while you're in Spain, and the Spanish are well known for their party-hard ways. But you don't have to limit your partying to bars and clubs, you can also explore Spain's very cool festival circuit. And the coolest festival of them all might just be the Monegros Desert Festival. This is an electronic music festival in the middle of the desert that attracts 40,000 people every year.

7. Discover Ancient History at the National Archaeological Museum of Spain

Established in 1867, the National Archaeology Museum of Spain is one of the world's premiere places to look at archaeological artefacts and learn about ancient history. The museum contains a staggering number of different objects. You'll get to see all kinds of artefacts from Ancient Islamic Spain, Ancient Egypt, Greek, Roman, Celtic periods, and much more besides. It's possible to spend more than a day exploring the collection, so take your time with it!

(Calle de Serrano, Madrid; www.man.es/man/home.html)

8. Sample Spanish Delicacies at Mercado de San Miguel

If you think of yourself as a bit of a foodie, there is one market that will totally bowl you over: Mercado de San Miguel in the centre of the city. The market structure of iron and glass is spectacular enough in its own right, but when you venture inside and start tasting the amazingness on offer, you'll want to stay inside all day. There are more than 30 carefully selected vendors, selling products such as authentic Spanish cheeses, olives, cured meats, and wines and cocktails. The vendors are also very eager to hand out free samples!

(Plaza de San Miguel, Madrid; www.mercadodesanmiguel.es/en)

9. Go Back to Medieval Spain at Granada's Alhambra

In our opinion, Granada is a must-visit city in the south of Spain, particularly if you are interested in grand architecture and the history of the country. And probably the most famous and important historic structure in Granada, and perhaps all of southern Spain, is the Alhambra, a stunning palace and fortress complex that was constructed in the mid 13th century by the Moorish

rulers of the time. The complex is huge, and you could easily spend a few days there walking around and taking all of its sumptuousness in.
(Calle Real de la Alhambra, s/n, 18009 Granada; www.alhambra-patronato.es)

10. Stroll Around the Botanical Gardens of Barcelona

Thanks to the wide, open streets of Barcelona, this is a city that feels very spacious, and not too crowded. But if you are somebody who needs lots of green and might feel overwhelmed by city life, somewhere you can escape to for a morning is the Botanical Gardens of Barcelona. The gardens specialise in plants from Mediterranean climates, with various sections such as Australia, Chile, California, and South Africa.
(Carrer del Doctor Font i Quer, 2, 08038 Barcelona; http://museuciencies.cat/visitans/jardi-botanic)

11. Visit an Egyptian Temple in Madrid

A temple from Ancient Egypt in the centre of Madrid? Yup! Unlikely as it may seem, the Temple of Debod was a temple from Egypt that was dismantled and then put back

together in the Spanish capital city. The temple dates right back to 200 BC, and was dedicated to the Goddess Isis. After the construction of the Aswan High Dam, the reservoir posed a threat to the temple, and it was consequently gifted to Madrid, and it now sits in the Parque del Oeste.
(Calle Ferraz, Madrid)

12. Look at Picasso's Guernica Up Close

There are a few paintings in the world that everyone has stored in the recess of the brain, whether they are an art fan or not. Picasso's Guernica, a painting that depicts an anti-war sentiment following the bombing of Guernica, is one such painting. Prints and reproductions of the painting can be found right across the globe, but there is only one place where you can see the real deal, and that's at the Museo Reina Sofia in Madrid.
(Calle de Santa Isabel; www.museoreniasofia.es/en)

13. Celebrate the Wine Harvest at the Haro Wine Festival

While you're in Spain it's imperative that you sip on at least a couple of the local wines. But if you are truly passionate about wine, we think that you should go one step further and find your way to the Haro Wine Festival, which is an annual celebration of the grape harvest in the La Rioja region in the north of Spain. It takes place on June 29th each year, and involves a procession through the streets, carrying a hell of a lot of red wine, and then the best part – drinking it!

14. Get to Grips with Village Life at Patones de Arriba

While Madrid is an exciting and dynamic city, if you have the urge to discover a slice of Spain that is a little more traditional and slower paced, you should absolutely take a day trip to Patones de Arriba. This is a village just 60km outside of the city, but it's a world away from the hustle and bustle of the Spanish capital. The village is said to be more than one thousand years old, and much of the architecture is slate, with an old, worn, but immensely charming feel. Walk the cobbled streets and pop into one of the bars for some tapas, and you'll feel instantly restored.

(Av. de Madrid, 71, 28189 Patones)

15. Enjoy a Snack of Almogrote on Toast in the Canaries

La Gomera is a little known island in the Canaries that people visit to enjoy the beaches and get away from it all. But we also think that it has some very spectacular cuisine, and Almogrote on toast is something that you are unlikely to find anywhere but on the island of La Gomera. It is a kind of terrine that is made from aged goat cheese, pepper, garlic, oil, and tomato, and it's then spread on toast. It's rich in flavour and perfect as a snack between meals at a beach bar.

16. Visit an Architectural Park Designed by Gaudi

Gaudi is, of course, one of the most beloved architects in Spain, and indeed the world. While in Barcelona, we advise looking beyond the Sagrada Familia and checking out some of his other more obscure works. Park Guell is a park with landscaping and architectural features that was created by Gaudi over the course of about 15 years, and it contains his trademark organic, swirling shapes. Inside, you can also find a house where the architect lived, and it's now the Gaudi House Museum.

(www.parkguell.cat)

17. Take in Iconic Moorish Architecture at the Mosque of Cordoba

While you are in Andalucía, there is no doubt that you will want to take in all the glory and grandeur of the ancient Moorish palaces, fortresses, and mosques. But we advise that you don't just stick to Granada and Seville, and that you find your way to the smaller and underrated city of Cordoba as well. It's here that you will find the Mosque of Cordoba, which is said to be the most important monument of the Western Islamic world. We would recommend hiring a guide to walk around with you, because knowing the history behind the opulence makes it all the more enjoyable.

(Calle del Cardenal Herrero, 1, 14003 Córdoba; https://mezquita-catedraldecordoba.es)

18. Stay in One of the Cave Houses of Guadix

To witness Spanish history right before your eyes or simply to take in a beautiful small city in the country, we would heartily recommend paying a visit to Guadix. Located in the province of Granada, this is considered one of the oldest human settlements in Spain. That sounds great on paper, but it's also astoundingly beautiful. One of the characteristic things about the city are the dwellings that are constructed into cave fronts. Some of these even operate as guesthouses, and it's a great way to experience this unique gem.

19. Cool Yourself Down With a Granizado

If you visit Spain during the summertime, you'll definitely be looking for some ways to cool down. Take a look around you and you'll see that one of the most popular ways for locals to cope with the heat is by slurping on a granizado. A granizado is essentially the Spanish version of a slushy, and it can come in a variety of delicious flavours. If you are wondering where to grab one for yourself, head to one of the many ice cream parlours around.

20. Lose Yourself in the Horta Labyrinth

Created all the way back in 1791, the Horta Labyrinth is the oldest garden to be found in Barcelona, and we'd say the grandest as well, giving a unique insight into the extravagances of the Spanish monarchy in Catalonia. The central element of the park is a labyrinth formation comprising two metre high hedges that link together to form a maze. Visiting this park is a charming way to enjoy history and the outdoors with kids.

(Passeig dels Castanyers, 1, 08035 Barcelona; http://guia.barcelona.cat/detall/parc-del-laberint-d-horta_92086011952.html)

21. Take a Long Hike From Beas de Granada to Granada

Spain is a country that has it all. You can see historic attractions, you can meet locals at banging parties, or you can simply immerse yourself in the stunning landscapes. If you are a nature lover, one of our favourite hikes in the Sierra Nevada is from Beas de Granada to the main city of Granada. At 16km, this is a long walk, but it's not especially difficult, and is very level throughout. You'll get a stunning view of the mountains, and we particularly like doing this hike in the winter when the hills are snow-capped.

22. Eat Delicious Pulpo a Feira While in Galicia

There is a hell of a lot of coastline around Spain, and this means that there is a hell of a lot of incredible seafood to be eaten. And because Spain is a large country, you can eat lots of different seafood dishes in different parts of the country. One of our favourite things to chow down on while we are in Galicia is something very special called Pulpo a Feira, which is octopus boiled in a copper pot and then sprinkled with salt, paprika, and olive oil. It's usually accompanied with red wine.

23. Immerse Yourself in Spanish Dance at the Annual Flamenco Festival

What is more Spanish than a live flamenco show? Well, at the annual flamenco festival you won't just get to see one flamenco performance, but hundreds! The Suma Flamenco Festival takes over Madrid every June, and you will have the opportunity to watch flamenco shows, from the traditional to the innovative, in ten boroughs across

the capital city. By the time you head home, you'll be a flamenco expert!
(www.madrid.org/sumaflamenca)

24. Be Wowed by the Toledo Cathedral

If you're a fan of religious architecture, there is plenty for you to see around Spain, and it's well worth finding your way to the small city of Toledo to check out its cathedral. This is one of the most impressive examples of Medieval Gothic architecture that we have ever seen. The exterior is grand and gorgeous, but the collection of art work inside is just as impressive, with works from the likes of Velazquez, Goya, and El Greco.
(Calle Cardenal Cisneros, 1, 45002 Toledo; www.catedralprimada.es)

25. Take a Cable Car to the Montserrat Abbey

While there is certainly lots to see and do in Barcelona, there are also some hidden gems dotted around the city that are worth exploring. And the Montserrat Abbey, which lies 45 kilometres outside of Barcelona, is certainly worth exploring in our opinion. This Benedictine abbey is located at the top of a 1200 metre high mountain. While there are walking trails to the top, we recommend taking the cable car for a more leisurely experience. The monastery also has a museum with works from the likes of Dali and Monet.

(Muntanya de Montserrat, 08199 Montserrat; www.abadiamontserrat.cat)

26. Explore the Old Arab Quarter of Granada, Albaycin

Of course, it can be great to seek out particular attractions like ancient palaces and beautiful churches, but sometimes we love nothing more than to walk around a quaint neighbourhood and take in the atmosphere. When we are in Granada, we always make sure that we etch a morning into our itineraries for nothing other than walking around Albaycin, an ancient Moorish neighbourhood that retains its original layout with quaint narrow streets. It's also at a height so you can check out sights like the Alhambra from the hilltop streets.

27. Visit a Ghost Metro Station

There is one metro station in Madrid unlike any of the others, Estacion de Chamberi. The station is something of local legend because most Madrid locals have never had the opportunity to alight at this station. It did, in fact, close its doors in 1966, and the station now serves as a museum/installation that recreates the inauguration of the station in 1919. You'll be able to see old train posters from the time, ticket offices, and other fascinating memorabilia.

28. Take in the Light Show of the Magic Fountain of Montjuic

To enjoy Barcelona, it's not necessary to spend lots of money on expensive tickets for shows or to empty your wallet at fancy cocktail bars because there are just as many free attractions. And something that never fails to make us feel all warm and fuzzy inside is the incredible light show of the Fountain of Montjuic. It was created in 1929 for the International Exhibition, and it has a display of music, water acrobatics, and lights of more than 50 colours.
(http://lameva.barcelona.cat/es/aprovechala/fuente-magica)

29. Indulge in a Big Bowl of Callos

Yes, there is yet more eating to do! You can't say that you have had the authentic Madrid experience until you have sat down with a steaming bowl of callos. This peasant dish may not be to everyone's tastes because the primary ingredient is tripe, but if you're down with offal, you are going to love it. The tripe is combined with chickpeas, blood sausage, chorizo, and a tomato and meat broth. It's the perfect dish for a winter's day, and it dates right back to the 15th century.

30. Let it All Hang Out at Barinatxe Beach

The Spanish are a pretty open minded set of people. Combine that with some glorious coastline, and what do you get? Nude beaches of course! If you're in the market for an all over tan, there are nude beaches in every single region of Spain, but we are really quite fond of Barinatxe Beach in the Province of Biscay. This is an extensive open beach that is shaded by cliffs, giving you the privacy that you might like if you do wish to take it all off.

31. Party While Finding a Bargain at Rave Market

Madrid has an exceptional market culture, and one of the most original markets in the city is Rave Market. Is it a rave or is it a market? Well, actually it's both. This market is held every month, and the location is usually in one of Madrid's wonderful concert venues. People are also encouraged to bring their own unwanted or used items and sell them – and all while dancing to pumping tunes from the DJ booth.

(http://theravemarket.com)

32. Enjoy All the Festivities of the Seville Fair

Semana Santa is one of the busiest and most festive times in Spain, but it's a couple of weeks after Easter that things really start to heat up in Seville because this is when the city hosts the Seville Fair. There is tonnes going on during the time of the fair; you can find fairground rides for all the family, horseback parades with female flamenco dancers, traditional bullfights, and some good old fashioned eating, drinking, and partying the night away in the streets.

(Calle Juan Belmonte, 38, 41011 Sevilla)

33. Have a Purse or Satchel Specially Made

In the historic centre of Madrid lies Taller Puntera, a workshop space that specialises in the production of hand crafted leather goods. You can simply buy one of their beautiful items off the shelf of the shop floor, but if you have a little bit more time, you can actually have something specially made. The artisans will talk you through all the options, from colours to shapes, sizes to the softness of the leather. Can you think of a better memory of Madrid from your trip?

(Plaza Conde de Barajas; www.puntera.com)

34. Be Wowed by Gaudi's Iconic Sagrada Familia

There are some buildings around the world that just everybody knows and can identify because they are that iconic. Gaudi's famous Sagrada Familia in Barcelona is most certainly one of those buildings. This Roman Catholic cathedral has been a work in progress for practically all of its existence, and at the time of Gaudi's death it was actually only about 25% complete. There's currently some building work happening on the site, but it's still a must visit while in Barcelona.

(Carrer de Mallorca, 401, 08013 Barcelona; www.sagradafamilia.org/index.html)

35. Eat in Picasso's Favourite Café

Barcelona has a thriving café culture, and there's no shortage of places where you can stop for a strong cup of coffee and a pastry, but there is no café that's quite like Els 4 Gats. This café opened in the latter half of the 19th century, and it quickly became a hangout and meeting place for Catalonia's Modernist artists like Pablo Picasso and Ramon Casas I Carbo. The poster that stands on the corner of the street outside of the café was designed by Picasso himself.

(Carrer de Montsió, 3, 08002 Barcelona; www.4gats.com)

36. Go Birdwatching in Donana National Park

Because of all of the incredible churches, fortresses, and museums, Spain can be somewhat neglected as a destination that is known for its natural beauty, but if you are the outdoorsy type, there are plenty of national parks to explore. For the most blissful quietude and some of the best birdwatching in Spain, we always like to go to the Donana National Park in Andalucia. More than half a million birds winter in the park, and half of Europe's bird species can be found there.

(www.mapama.gob.es)

37. Join in With Madrid's Gay Pride Festivities

Madrid is one of the most gay friendly cities in the world, and this is never more evident than during the Gay Pride celebrations that occur at the end of June or beginning of July each year. There are tonnes of parties in the city's happening gay clubs, but the highlight has to be the main parade, with hundreds of floats that navigate their way through the city streets as merry makers cheer them on and wave their rainbow flags with pride. Why not be a part of the celebrations?

(www.madridorgullo.com)

38. Sip on a Traditional Seville Cocktail, Rebujito

Down in Andalucía, the temperatures really soar in the summer months, and one of our favourite ways to cool down is with a refreshing cocktail that is native to Seville: the Rebujito. Sherry is one of the most popular tipples in the south of the country, and in this simple but refreshing cocktail, it's sherry that's the star of the show. Combine the sherry with ginger ale and a few sprigs of mint, and you have something to get you through the Spanish heat in the most delightful way.

39. Take a Day Trip to El Escorial

If you have filled your boots with sightseeing inside Madrid and you are looking for a little bit of tranquillity, El Escorial makes for a great day trip as it's less than an hour away. El Escorial is a historic residence of the King of Spain, and it functions as a royal palace, a museum, a school, and a convent all in one. With so much to see and explore, it's more than possible to spend the entire day here and really immerse yourself in the stunning Spanish gothic architecture of the buildings.

(Av Juan de Borbón y Battemberg, s/n, 28200 San Lorenzo de El Escorial; http://el-escorial.com)

40. Shop for Treasures at Barcelona Vintage Market

While you are in Spain, there's no doubt that you will want to take back some treasures that will always remind you of your trip. Our advice would be to avoid the shops that are specifically targeted towards tourists, and head to some of the local markets instead – and there are plenty of them! Our top tip for Barcelona is the Barcelona Vintage Market. You'll find everything from vintage furniture to antique jewellery and vinyl records. So get shopping. *(www.barcelonavintagemarket.com)*

41. Enjoy the Wild Isolated Beach of Langre in Cantabria

If you love nothing more than to lie on the beach, top up your tan, and watch the waves lap against the shore, Spain is one of the best destinations in Europe to visit. There are many beaches to choose from, but if you want to find something a little off the beaten track, the Cantabria region in the northern Basque country is less exploited by tourism than the south. Our favourite beach there is called Langre, which has a wild and unspoiled feel. It's also a great spot for surfing.

42. Go Back in Time at the Prehistory Museum of Valencia

History buffs need to etch a trip to the Prehistory Museum of Valencia into their diaries as a matter of priority. The Roman history of the city can be seen all around Valencia in the city walls and gates, but what about life in Valencia before then? This museum will give you a peek into that life right from the origins of Homo Sapiens in the area. The museum collections consists of many bones, remains, coins, tools, and dug out excavations from many centuries ago.

(Centro Cultural La Beneficència, Carrer de la Corona, 36, 46003 Valencia; www.museuprehistoriavalencia.es/web_mupreva)

43. Hike Pico Sobarcal on the French Border

Spain is a country with incredible amounts to offer in terms of nature and landscapes, and if you do enjoy a day hike to get you breathy, we recommend the north of the country where you can find Pico Sobarcal on the border of France. The hike takes around seven hours and towards the top it can be quite challenging with lots of rockiness, but we assure you that you'll have a spectacular view of the Pyrenees at the top.

44. Eat the Best Paella of Your Life in Valencia

Is there any food that screams "Spain!" more than a heaped bowlful of paella? Probably not, right? And while it certainly is the case that you can taste awesome plates of paella all around the country, we think it's well worth seeking out a yummy plate of the good stuff in the birthplace of the dish: Valencia. And our restaurant of choice is Restaurante Levante. It also has a cellar with more than 10,000 wines, which is no bad thing.

(Carrer de Góngora, 1, 46015 València; www.restaurantelevante.com)

45. Explore a Gorgeous Moorish Palace in Seville

Seville is a must-visit destination in Spain for all fans of architecture and history. The region of Andalucía is a place that has incredible amount of history dating back to the Moorish period, and the palaces and mosques are representative of that. The 1300s are sometimes known as the Dark Ages of Europe, but when you see this fortress complex in Seville from that period you are sure to think otherwise. It was quite rightly declared a World Heritage Site in 1987.

(Patio de Banderas, s/n, 41004 Sevilla; www.alcazarsevilla.org)

46. Get Artsy at the Castile-Leon International Arts Festival

If you are the artsy type, you will have a whale of a time hopping from gallery to gallery and checking out traditional dance, but something else that you might want to do is go to one of the local arts festivals, and a festival that all artsy Spanish types try to attend is the Castile-Leon International Arts Festival, hosted each June in Salamanca. This festival is primarily concerned with performances, but all types, so whether you would like to see some contemporary dance, performance art, or circus performances, this is the place to be.

(www.facyl.com)

47. Visit an 18th Century Olive Oil Mill

For those with leanings towards gastronomical experiences, Spain is a must visit country, and there is loads more to do than eat paella and drink some wine. If you are a true foodie, it can be a wonderful idea to actually learn about the food culture, and what better way to do exactly that than to make your way to an 18th century olive oil mill? El Vinculo has tours from Monday to Saturday with tastings of bread and their oils.

(Crta. Zahara - Grazalema s/n, 11688 Zahara de la Sierra; www.molinoelvinculo.com)

48. Cool Yourself Down With Salmorejo in Cordoba

The south of the country gets astoundingly hot in the summer months, and you'll want to take every possible opportunity to cool down. Of course, there's bottles of water and air conditioning, but a far more enjoyable way of cooling down is by slurping on a bowl of Salmorejo, a chilled soup that comes from the city of Cordoba. All it consists of is tomatoes, bread, garlic, and olive oil that is whizzed up. It differs from gazpacho because of its much thicker consistency.

49. Embrace Your Inner Bookworm at the National Library

The Bibiloteca Nacional is one of the most important and beautiful buildings in Madrid. It is now over 300 years old, and it's the largest library in Spain, and one of the largest in the whole world. A visit here is a bibliophile's dream.

There are interactive displays about the Spanish printing presses, illuminated manuscripts, and literary cafes inside the building where you can relax with a cup of coffee and a great book.

(Paseo de Recoletos, Bilbao; www.bne.es)

50. Discover a World of Modern Art at the Guggenheim Museum of Bilbao

Art lovers will be in paradise on their trip to Spain. It's more than possible to spend an entire trip ambling from museum to museum and gallery to gallery across various cities in the country, and no artsy trip to Spain would be complete without visiting the Guggenheim Museum of Bilbao. This is an incredible building in its own right, but the exhibitions are just as impressive. Some of the artists on display include Yves Klein, David Hockney, and Mark Rothko.

(Abandoibarra Etorb., 2, 48009 Bilbo; www.guggenheim-bilbao.eus)

51. Listen to a Classical Concert at the Auditorio Nacional

Madrid is a wonderful place to soak up some culture. Once you are done with a day of looking at religious buildings and exploring museums, you can relax into a cultural evening of classical music at the Auditorio Nacional. It is the residence of both the National Orchestra of Spain and the Symphony Orchestra of Madrid, so you are practically guaranteed that any performance here will be world class.

(Calle del Príncipe de Vergara; www.auditorionacional.mcu.es)

52. Visit an Innovative Winery, Bodegas Protos

If you are a wine lover, you might think about visiting France before you visit Spain, but with its Mediterranean climate, there's also some incredible wines to be enjoyed in Spain, and you could quite easily make a whole vacation out of exploring the wine country. But if you only have time to visit one winery on your trip, we would be sure to make it Bodegas Protos. All the grapes are handpicked, the wines are award winning, and it also has a stunning futuristic construction that you wouldn't typically associate with a winery.

(Camino Bodegas Protos, 24-28, 47300 Peñafiel; www.bodegasprotos.com/en)

53. Learn How to Surf in Concha Bay

When you think of places around the world where you could have a surfing adventure, you might think of the coast of Bali or the Mexican Pacific, but Spain has its fair share of waves too, and whether you are a beginner or a seasoned surfer, the beach you need to know about is Concha Bay up in the Basque Country. There are quite a few surf schools there that can take you through the whole process and rent any equipment you might need.

54. Feast on Calamari Sandwiches

One thing that's a guarantee on your trip to Madrid is that you will eat exceptionally well. And the nice thing about Madrid is that it doesn't matter what your budget is, you'll find some incredible food to match your wallet regardless. And if you are looking for cheap eats, you can't do much better than the delicious calamari sandwiches that can be found across the city. The calamari is breaded, fried, and placed inside a fluffy bread roll. Ideal hangover food, and a restaurant called La Ideal is said to serve up the best calamari sandwiches in the city.

(Calle Botoneras, 4, 28012 Madrid;
https://www.facebook.com/bar.la.ideal)

55. Get to Grips With Basque Culture at Musee Basque

The north of Spain is extremely underrated in our opinion, and we love spending time in Spain where the country borders France to really immerse ourselves in the unique Basque culture of the region. And a must-visit place if you really want to get to grips with Basque culture is the Basque Museum in Bilbao. It has more than 20,000 objects that reflects the daily life and work of Basque people in history and today.

(Unamuno Miguel Plaza, 4, 48006 Bilbo; www.euskal-museoa.eus/en/hasiera)

56. Go Ham Crazy at Museo del Jamon

While in Madrid, you'll want to put as much food in your mouth as humanly possible, and the hams and cured meats are a definite highlight. Museo del Jamon is something of a Madrid institution, and tourists are often taken by the sight of the multiple cured hams hanging from the ceilings. If

you are a cinema fan, you may even recognise this sight from the Almodovar movie, Live Flesh. Prices start at a very reasonable 2.50 euros for a simple ham roll, but we have the feeling that you'll be sticking around and sampling a lot more. Their sangria is also delicious!
(Calle de Atocha; http://museodeljamon.es)

57. Discover Spanish Fashion and Costumes at Museo del Traje

As you walk around Madrid's streets, you can't fail to notice how chic the local population looks, but when you visit the Museo del Traje, you'll begin to appreciate the influence of Spanish fashion, clothing, and costumes across a much longer expanse of time. The collection here contains a staggering 160,000 items, with clothing from the Middle Ages right up to works from Spanish fashion designers creating garments today.
(Av. Juan de Herrera; http://museodeltraje.mcu.es)

58. Brush Up Your Spanish Skills

When you visit any country, it's a great idea to know at least the basics of a language so that you can understand some of what's happening around you and form deeper connections. Fortunately, Spanish is one of the easiest languages to learn, and there are tonnes of Spanish schools all over the country. If you have time to spare and fancy spending a week or a month in language school, we'd recommend the Agualivar School in Lagos for its stunning views out on to the ocean.

(Las chorreras, 73, 29760 Lagos, Málaga; http://spanishinagualivar.com)

59. Be Stunned by an Ancient Muslim Palace in Granada

If it's ancient Moorish architecture that you want to see while you're in Spain, Andalucía is of course the region that you need to spend plenty of time in. Seville is the obvious spot, but be sure to make it to Granada as well. We always think that "Generalife" sounds like the name of a terrible health insurance company, but it is in fact a sumptuous summer palace built by the Nasrid rulers of Granada. It was built in the 14th century and consists of a long pool covered by flowerbeds, colonnades, fountains, and pavilions.

(www.alhambra-patronato.es/index.php/The-Generalife/31/0)

60. Eat in the World's Oldest Restaurant!

There are endless opportunities for great dining in the Spanish capital, but one of the most special of them all has to be Restaurant Botin. Why is this place such a must visit restaurant? Because it's officially the oldest restaurant in the world according the Guinness World Records. Restaurant Botin first opened its doors in 1725, which is almost 300 years ago! Since then, it has been serving up traditional Spanish dishes to hungry locals, and you won't want to miss their roast suckling pig.

(Calle Cuchilleros; www.botin.es/en)

61. Visit a Landmark of Malaga, the Alcazaba

Malaga is a port city on the Costa de Sol that's very popular with holidaymakers who want to relax with sunshine, beach time, and cocktails. But if those lazy beach days start to wear thin, there are also historic attractions in Malaga, and one of the most impressive of them all is the city's Alcazaba or citadel. The palace fortress dates way back to the 11th century with beautiful courtyards, arches, fountains, and the scent of jasmine and orange blossoms throughout.

(Calle Alcazabilla, 2, 29012 Málaga; www.malagaturismo.com/es/recursos-turisticos/detalle/alcazaba/6)

62. Take a Street Art Tour of Madrid

In order to really understand a city, it's important to get beyond what exists behind glass containers in museums, and actually feel the lifeblood of a city on the streets. A way of appreciating Madrid's artistic counterculture is by paying attention to the art that is painted on to the city's walls. You are most likely to see Madrid's street art in the outer suburbs of the city, and it's a great idea to take a guided street art tour so that you can really appreciate the political messages and the creative skill that go into the wall murals you might otherwise walk right past.

63. Keep Kids Entertained at the City of Arts & Sciences

Travelling with kids is a double edged sword. On the one hand it's a huge privilege to be able to provide your children with memories that they'll treasure for years and years to come, but on the other hand it can be very difficult to keep kids entertained. That's why we love the City of Arts & Sciences in Valencia, a place where kids can learn something new and have fun at the same time. The highlight has to be Europe's largest aquarium with 45,000 specimens of 500 different sea creatures.

(Av. del Professor López Piñero, 7, 46013 València; www.cac.es/es/home.html)

64. Have a Snorkelling Adventure Off Tabarca Island

If you are the kind of person who prefers to get to know a country by getting stuck into its landscapes than by ambling from museum to museum, we'd love to suggest having an underwater adventure while you're on the coast. There are quite a few places where you can try out snorkelling or diving, but our favourite is Tabarca Island, a little islet in the province of Alicante. The cleanness of the water attracts divers from all over, so don't forget to pack your goggles.

65. Stroll the Aisles of Europe's Biggest Indoor Market, Mercado de la Ribera

One of the best ways of getting to know a local culture is by strolling the aisles of its markets, talking to the vendors, having a bite to eat, and picking up some lovely things to take home. Spain has a thriving market culture, and we are particularly fond of the Mercado de la Ribera in Bilbao, which with a space of 10,000 square metres is the largest covered market in all of Europe. There's a good selection of pintxos bars inside – ideal for when your feet are weary from sightseeing and you need a pick-me-up.
(Erribera Kalea, s/n, 48005 Bilbo; www.mercadodelaribera.net)

66. Throw Some Tomatoes at the Tomatina Festival

One of the best ways to get to grips with any local culture is by attending a local festival and joining in with the celebrations. The Tomatina Festival is something very unique, and if you don't mind getting messy, we think that you'll have the time of your life there. The festival is hosted in the Valencian town of Bunol on the last Wednesday of August. The basic idea is that everyone throws tomatoes at each other on the street. It stems from 1945 when political protestors through tomatoes at buildings and officials, but now it's purely a fun-filled time on the streets of Spain.

(http://latomatina.info/en)

67. Have a Lusty Afternoon in Barcelona's Erotic Museum

Barcelona has many standout attractions, which make it the go-to destination of Europe, but we have been to Barcelona so many times that we really like to get off the beaten track and check out some of the attractions that are more hidden away. Take the Erotic Museum, for example, which is ideal when you're in a bit of a lusty mood. It contains 800 objects that relate to eroticism right from Ancient Rome and Greece and up to the present day.

(La Rambla, 96 bis, 08002 Barcelona; www.erotica-museum.com)

68. Go Fly Fishing on the River Cares

The Asturius region in the northwest of Spain is a place that you might not have even heard of before, but that's all the more reason to visit in our opinion. And if your idea of a great vacation isn't museum hopping or seeing grand churches but sitting at the edge of a river with a fishing rod, this is truly a must visit place. In the River

Caras, you can find monkfish, conger eel, red mullet, bream, and more. Perhaps you'll even catch your dinner.

69. Have an Exquisite Evening at Barcelona's Tandem Cocktail Bar

Let's face it, you aren't going to have too much trouble finding a wonderful place to have a drink or two in Barcelona, but actually, there is so much choice that it can be overwhelming. When we are pondering where to go for a cocktail, Tandem Cocktail Bar is always a safe bet. This is an old school place with bartenders dressed up in white shirts and black jackets. But it's not all for show – the drinks are just as snazzy, and we are particularly fond of their Gin Fizz.

(Carrer d'Aribau, 86, 08036 Barcelona; www.tandemcocktail.com)

70. Take in a Traditional Zarzuela Performance

Almost everybody around the world has heard about Spanish flamenco dancing, but what about zarzuela? This form of Spanish performance isn't quite so celebrated, but it's well worth catching a show on your visit to Madrid, and the impressive Teatro de Zarzuela is the place to do so. Zarzuela is a type of musical theatre that switches between spoken and sung scenes. While the lyrics will be in Spanish, it's worth visiting for the stunning visuals and the atmosphere alone. There are also contemporary dance performances at the Teatro de Zarzuela if that is more your thing.

(Calle de Jovellanos; http://teatrodelazarzuela.mcu.es/en)

71. Take in the View of Valencia from Torres de Serranos

As you walk the streets of Valencia, you are sure to notice that it's a city of contrasts. You can see very modern buildings right next to buildings that have been standing for centuries upon centuries, and one of the historic highlights of the city has to be the Torres de Serranos, one of twelve gates that forms the Ancient city all built way back in the 14th century. You can walk right to the top of the towers where you'll have incredible views right out over the city.

(Plaça dels Furs, s/n, 46003 València)

72. Party in the Street at Barcelona's La Merce Festival

Barcelona is a fantastic party city at absolutely any time of the year, but it's at the end of September that Barcelona feels particularly festive for the annual La Merce Festival, which takes place on September 24th every year. The festival is a celebration of Barcelona's Patron Saint, Virgin de la Merce, with many fun events including a procession of giant wooden figures through the city.

73. Chow Down on Pig's Ear

If you really want to eat like one of the locals on your trip to Madrid, there's one dish that you simply have to try at least once: pig's ear. And no, it's not a euphemism for something a little more delicate, we're literally talking about chowing down on the ear of a pig here. So the ear of a pig is fried, and sometimes onions and mushrooms are included as well. Wash it down with a cold glass of beer and you'll survive to tell the tale!

74. Ogle the Surrealist Sculptures at Parc de Joan Miro

Barcelona is one of those cities that just has it all. As well as incredible shopping streets, wonderful eateries, and beaches, there's also an abundance of green spaces, and one of the most unique green spaces that you will find in Barcelona is the Parc de Joan Miro, which unsurprisingly is a park that contains sculptures created by Miro. There's also plenty of green space, so why not pack a picnic, and enjoy a leisurely day in the Spanish sunshine?

(Carrer d'Aragó, 2, 08015 Barcelona; http://lameva.barcelona.cat/es/aprovechala/parques-y-jardines/parque-de-joan-miro_92086012013.html)

75. Top up a Tan at Es Pujols, Formentera

The best known island of the Balearics is certainly Ibiza, but if you're not so much of a party-hopper, the sister island of Formentera is a wonderful alternative for long and lazy days on the beach without banging club music or excessive boozing. And our favourite beach on this island would have to be Es Pujols. It's a smallish place where you'll get to know the locals with a cocktail, and the sand is perfectly fine and white.

76. Relax in a Traditional Hammam in Cordoba

If you want to learn about the history of southern Spain but you don't have the energy to take in yet another museum or grand mosque, then we would recommend visiting the Hammam Arab baths of Cordoba, where you can immerse yourself in the Arab history of the region while indulging in a completely relaxing experience. These baths dates back to the Al Andalus Kingdom, but have been renovated so that you can use them today. There is a hot bath, a cold bath, a steam room, and an area for massages, hot stones, and other treatments.

(C/ Corregidor Luis de la Cerda, 51, 14003 Córdoba; http://cordoba.hammamalandalus.com/en)

77. Take in a Free Movie at Cineteca Madrid

Amidst all of your sightseeing, there might be a time when you simply want to kick back with a good movie. Cineteca, a cultural centre in Madrid, is the place to do so. They err on the side of documentaries, and most of the screenings here are free, so this is also the ideal place to save your pennies. There are also cultural activities such as exhibition openings, performances, and lectures, as well as a rather lovely restaurant and bar that serves up local beers from Madrid.

(Plaza de Legazpi; www.cinetecamadrid.com)

78. Get to Grips With Barcelona's History at Museu d'Historia de Barcelona

Barcelona is a city that has it all. If you want to walk the streets and look at the architecture, or if you want to eat lots of pinchos and drink sangria, you can do it. And if you want more of a cultural trip, there's also a fantastic museum scene, and we'd advise going to the Museu d'Historia de Barcelona which tells the story of Barcelona from Roman times and up to the present day. One of the obscure highlights we love is the remains of a Roman salt fish and garum factory.

(Plaça del Rei, s/n, 08002 Barcelona; http://museuhistoria.bcn.cat)

79. Dance, Dance, Dance at Bilbao BBK Live

One of the greatest things about Spain in the summertime is that there are countless summer festivals to choose from, and there is something for you whether you're into

rock, jazz, or classical music. One of the most enduringly popular festivals takes place in Bilbao each July and is called Bilbao BBK Live. Some of the world famous acts that have taken to the stage include Keane, The Cure, Radiohead, Mumford & Sons, and Garbage.
(http://bilbaobbklive.com/en-us/home)

80. Chow Down on Bombas While in Barcelona

Bomba is an interesting word in Barcelona. It literally means "bomb", it can also be used as a slang word that means something along the lines of "cool", and it is also a local type of food in Barcelona that we just can't get enough of. These little bombs are essentially a mix of meat and potatoes that are deep fried and slathered in tomato sauce. They are filling and a slightly different taste of Spain that you will only find in Barcelona.

81. Tuck Into Catalonia's Finest Cheeses at Formatgeria la Seu

If you are a cheese lover, you might first think of visiting France before you head to Spain, but there is more than enough in Spain to keep cheese lovers happy, and as with many things in Spain, each region has different types of local cheeses. To explore the local cheese of Catalonia, we'd recommend visiting a Barcelona cheesemonger called Formatgeria la Seu. It sells only carefully selected produce from small farms, and do check in with them to see if you can catch one of their wine and cheese tastings.

82. Be Wowed by the Royal Palace of Madrid

The official residence of the Spanish Royal family, the Royal Palace of Madrid is arguably the most important building in the entire country. The palace dates back to the latter half of the 18th century, and with a staggering 3418 rooms, this is the largest Royal Palace in all of Europe. The palace is impressive enough from the outside, but it's also possible to enter and walk around its hallways and rooms where you'll be able to spot artworks from Caravaggio, Valezquez, Goya, and many other prominent European artists. Don't miss the Royal Armoury, which contains one of the most comprehensive armoury collections in the world, with pieces dating back to the 13th century.

(Calle de Bailén; www.patrimonionacional.es)

83. Allow the Cascada de Ezaro Waterfall to Take Your Breath Away

What is more special than looking at swathes of water cascading down a waterfall? Well, there's more than a few waterfalls around Spain that are sure to take your breath away, and perhaps our favourite of them all is the Cascada de Ezaro, which is pretty much located in the middle of nowhere, and that's what makes it all the more special. This is also a unique place because the waterfalls flows from the river and directly into the sea.

84. Take in a Concert at a Stunning Barcelona Concert Hall

Barcelona is a great place for budget travellers because simply walking the streets and taking in the incredible architecture is a wonderful attraction in itself. One of our favourite buildings is a 19th century concert hall called the Palau de la Musica Catalana, and it has been constructed in a Catalan Modernist style with swirls and dynamic forms taking precedence over straight lines. And if you did have a little money left in your budget, do take in a live concert there for an unforgettable experience.

(C/ Palau de la Música, 4-6, 08003 Barcelona; www.palaumusica.cat)

85. Visit a Traditional Cider House in the Basque Country

What to drink while you're in Spain? Well, actually there are countless options. There are some wonderful Spanish wines, both wine and red, and Spain has a thriving beer culture too. Something that you might not expect to find in Spain is cider, but there is actually quite a lot of cider to be found when you head north into the Basque country. There are many traditional cider houses to visit, and one we would recommend is Lizeaga. It has a hearth for the winter months, and their ribs are also delicious.

(Martutene Pasealekua, 139, 20014 San Sebastián; www.lizeaga.eus)

86. Find a Bargain at El Rastro Flea Market

El Rastro is a Madrid institution. Every Sunday, this open air market attracts thousands of visitors along Plaza de Cascorro. The space is truly gargantuan, and over 3500 stalls can be held here every week, which is fantastic news for bargain hunters on a trip to Madrid. At El Rastro, you can find all kinds of goodies, from vintage furniture through to hand made pieces of jewellery. Just be sure to have Google Maps switched on because it's all too easy to get lost!

(Calle de la Ribera de Curtidores, Madrid)

87. Discover Ancient Cave Art in El Castillo Cave

Spain is well known as a country that has had a varied an interesting history, from the civil war through to the Arab occupation of Andalucía, but if you are a true history buff, you have the opportunity to go back even further in time on your trip to Spain by visiting the El Castillo Cave, which contains the oldest cave art known to man. Enter the cave and you'll find prehistoric dots and bright red hand stencils that indicate that the Neanderthals were the world's first artists.

(SP-6022, s/n, 39670 Puente Viesgo, Cantabria;
http://cuevas.culturadecantabria.com/el-castillo/horarios-y-tarifas)

88. Hike Through the Volcanic Vineyards of Lanzarote

Let's face it. When you think about the island of Lanzarote, you probably think of cheap package holidays and 20 year olds getting super drunk at night, and while that does exist on Lanzarote, it is far from the whole story. In fact, Lanzarote has an incredibly unique landscape because it's a volcanic island, and this means it has incredible soil for vineyards. It is possible to hike through the volcanic vineyards, which are spectacularly scenic, and, of course, sip on some local wine en route.

89. Tuck Into Traditional Barcelona Tapas at Euskal Etxea

Barcelona is a delightful city for filling your stomach, and no trip to Barcelona would be complete without filling up on pintxos, which are essentially small plates, or tapas. And our favourite places for pintxos while we're in the city is a local haunt called Euskal Etxea. Almost everything consists of something atop a slice of crusty bread, whether it's a slice of cheese, a type of ham, or some kind of seafood. It's simple, yes, but it totally works. Their ciders are also worth a try.

(Placeta de Montcada, 1, 08003 Barcelona; http://gruposagardi.com/restaurante/euskal-etxea-taberna)

90. Visit an Ancient Roman Theatre in Merida

The Romans were an incredible force in prehistory, but we don't often hear that much about the Roman influence in Spain. That, however, will no longer be the case if you make it to Merida, an underrated city in western central Spain. It's here that you can find an Ancient Roman theatre that is actually still in pretty good condition considering that it dates back to 16 BC. There is also a classical theatre festival in Merida if you'd like to see this glorious Roman monument in use.

(Plaza Margarita Xirgu, s/n, 6800 Mérida; www.consorciomerida.org/conjunto/monumentos/teatro)

91. Visit the Birthplace of Pablo Picasso in Malaga

Picasso is not only one of the most celebrated artists from Spain, but that the world has ever produced, and for us, a trip to Spain is never complete without a little injection of Picasso. Of course, there is the stunning Picasso Museum in Barcelona, but if you fancy something a little off the beaten track, you can actually visit the birthplace of the man himself in the southern city of Malaga. Inside, you'll learn about the early life of the man, as well as see some of his rarer sketches and paintings.

(Plaza de la Merced, 15, 29012 Málaga; http://fundacionpicasso.malaga.eu)

92. Enjoy a Typical Valencian Dish, Esgarrat

Spain is a country that varies wildly from region to region, in terms of culture, language, landscapes, and of course, food. When we are in Valencia, we also like to seek out the scrumptious local dishes, and our favourite thing to eat in Valencia might just be Esgarrat, something that is rarely found outside of the region. It's a refreshing treat comprising of salt cod, grilled red peppers, olives, garlic, and olive oil.

93. Get Moving at the Tenerife Walking Festival

Tenerife is not only an island where you go for a package holiday with all you can drink swim up bars – it's actually far prettier than you have ever imagined! And one of the very best ways to get acquainted with all of the stunning beauty of the island is to head to Tenerife at the end of May, when they have a four day walking festival each year.

Bring your hiking boots, enjoy the landscapes, and meet other like minded hikers.

(www.tenerifewalkingfestival.com/en)

94. Visit a Village That's Built into Its Rock Formations

Spain is one of those travel destinations that everyone seems to know a little bit about. And with such world class cities like Madrid, Barcelona, and Seville that should hardly come as any sort of surprise. But if you are already acquainted with the main tourist haunts, it's worth getting off the beaten path and exploring some of the less visited towns and villages. Take Margalef, for example. This is an isolated village that's literally built into rock formations, so walking around is a very unique experience.

95. Party in the Open Air at Barcelona's La Terrrazza

The Barcelona sunshine is one of our favourite things in the entire world. It's a place where it's typically sunny throughout the year, and even in the winter time it's not particularly cold. And our favourite way of enjoying the sunshine of Barcelona is by partying in the open air at La

Terrrazza. Head there in the early evening if you want a quiet cocktail, or arrive after midnight if you want to party hard into the night in the balmy open air of Catalonia.

(Avenida Francesc Ferrer I Guardia, 0 S N (Poble Espanyol), 08001 Barcelona; http://laterrrazza.com)

96. Go Back in Time at the Archaeological Museum of Seville

Seville is one of the cities that history buffs simply have to visit. As well as visiting the many mosques and fortresses from the Moorish period, it can be great idea to have an afternoon of learning at the Archaeological Museum of Seville. The difference is that this museum starts in prehistory and ends with the Moorish period. One of the highlights is the Carambolo treasure from the Tartessian period.

(Plaza América, s/n, 41013 Sevilla; www.museosdeandalucia.es/cultura/museos/MASE/index.jsp?redirect=S2_3_1.jsp)

97. Sip on Sherries at a Sherry Bodega, Tio Pepe

If you make it down to Andalucía, something that you need to try before you leave is sherry, a type of fortified sweet white wine that is only made in this part of Spain. Of course, you will be able to order sherry in any bar in the region, but for an even more special experience it's a great idea to head to a sherry bodega like Bodega Tio Pepe, which is a magnificent traditional bodega spread across three floors.

(Calle Manuel María González, 12, 11403 Jerez de la Frontera, Cádiz; https://bodegastiopepe.com)

98. Walk Through the Sewers of Barcelona

As you walk along the wide, tree lined streets of Barcelona, you will only see a very polished city with a reputation for being one of the most liveable places on the planet. But there is an underside to this city that you won't see as you walk around. Believe it or not, the 19th century sewers, the foundations of which were laid in the Medieval period, are open to the public for exploration. As you are guided around, you'll get to know the history of the tunnels, of sanitation in Barcelona, and of folklore relating to the sewers.

99. Visit an Old Mosque School in Granada

If you are visiting the region of Andalucia, it's impossible to ignore the profound affect that the Moorish people and their Muslim religion had on Spain in the Middle Ages. As well as palaces and fortresses, you can find beautiful mosque schools, such as the Madrasah of Granada. It was founded in 1349 by the Nasrid monarch at the time. Back then, it was set in the heartland of the city, next to a bazaar where silk, gold, linen, and other valuable commodities were traded. Many subjects were studied at the school, including theology, law, medicine, astronomy, and more.
(Calle Oficios, 14, 18001 Granada; http://lamadraza.ugr.es)

100. Indulge With a Catalan Dessert, Mato

There is a huge amount of culinary treats to enjoy while in Spain, but what if you have a sweet tooth and you're more interested in dulces than meats and cheeses? Well, you're not left out either, we can assure you of that. And if you find yourself in the Catalonian part of Spain, one of the treats that you will surely want to enjoy is called Mato. This dessert is super simple, but so delicious. It consists of unsalted goats cheese, drizzled with honey, and then topped with toasted walnuts.

101. Swim Through Europe's First Underwater Museum

Spain is a country with no shortage of museums. There are incredible art galleries, anthropology museums, science museums, museums for kids, and more. But one of the most unusual museums in Spain, and indeed anywhere, has to be the Museo Atlantico situated on the island of Lanzarote. So what's the big deal? Well instead of walking through the aisles of the museum, this is a museum that you actually swim through while discovering the underwater sculptures. If you're a water-baby, this is definitely one to try.

(Puerto Marina Rubicón, Calle el Berrugo, 2, 35580 Playa Blanca, Las Palmas; www.cactlanzarote.com/cact/museo-atlantico)

Before You Go

Thanks for reading **101 Amazing Things to Do in Spain.** We hope that it makes your trip a memorable one!

Have a great trip, and don't eat too much paella!

Team 101 Amazing Things

Made in the USA
Coppell, TX
13 December 2022